HOW TO BE SCHOOL SMART

SUPER STUDY SKILLS

REVISED EDITION

Elizabeth James and Carol Barkin

Beech Tree
New York

(Previous edition published as
How to Be School Smart: Secrets of Successful Schoolwork)

For Elsa DeVita, Jeri Waldman, Bruce Crandall,
Mike Eckelman, and all the others who shared their
knowledge and expertise with us

Published by Lothrop, Lee & Shepard Books
an imprint of Morrow Junior Books
a division of William Morrow and Company, Inc.
1350 Avenue of the Americas, New York, NY 10019
www.williammorrow.com

Printed in the United States of America.

The Library of Congress has cataloged the Lothrop, Lee & Shepard Books version of *How to Be School Smart* as follows:
James, Elizabeth.
How to be school smart: super study skills / Elizabeth James and Carol Barkin.—Rev. ed.
p. cm.
Includes index.
ISBN 0-688-16130-8
1. Study skills—Juvenile literature. 2. Homework—Juvenile literature. 3. Students—Time management—Juvenile literature.
I. Barkin, Carol. II. Title. LB1601.J36 1998 371.3'028'1—dc21
98-14940 CIP AC

Revised Beech Tree Edition, 1998
ISBN 0-688-16139-1

10 9 8 7

CONTENTS

CHAPTER 1

STEPS TO SUCCESS

WHAT DO YOU WANT IN SCHOOL? How about straight A's on your report card and a way to learn everything you need to know quickly and easily? Probably everyone wants school to be like this. But no one thinks it can actually happen.

Of course, no method of approaching schoolwork can guarantee that you will get straight A's. But the ideas in this book really will help you learn to study more efficiently and to take tests without panicking. You'll be able to organize yourself and find time for all your homework, as well as for the other things you want to do. You'll discover the style of learning that works best for you so you can make the most of your study time. And you'll relax about tests and quizzes once you master the tips and hints revealed in these pages.

As you get older and move up through the grades in school, it's exciting to find new areas of knowledge opening up to you. But sometimes it can be kind of confusing and even a little scary. Probably you have more homework now than ever before; often you may feel as if you don't know where to begin. And when you're faced with difficult tests, you may get so worried that you can't even think.

This book will help! The ideas and techniques in these pages will allow you to focus on doing your best work at home and in class. When you uncover the terrific student you truly are, you'll have a head start on success in school.

CHAPTER 2

ORGANIZING YOUR STUDY SPACE

"**Y**OU'VE GOT TO GET ORGANIZED!" How many times have you told yourself that, or had someone else say it to you? It sounds like a good idea, but it's not always so easy to do. How can you get started?

Most people feel that it's helpful to have a special place where you do your studying. The idea is to train your brain so that every time you plop down in your study space, your mind clicks in and says, "Time to study!"

Of course, your study space may not be exactly like someone else's. If you have your own bedroom, your study space might be in one corner, with a desk, a chair, and a bulletin board. What if you share a room with a younger brother or sister who goes to bed early? Maybe you can make a study space somewhere else in the house, like the family room or the kitchen. Ask your mom and dad for suggestions. Even a card table that you set up in the living room every afternoon can be a perfectly fine study space.

ESSENTIAL EQUIPMENT

What does your study space need to contain? First, good light. Whatever kind of homework you are doing, you need light that makes it easy to see the work and doesn't make you squint. Some people like to have a lot of light when they study. Are you someone who turns on the overhead light in the room and all the lamps as well? Or do you prefer a less bright room and a warm pool of light from your reading lamp? Try to arrange the lighting in your study space the way you like it—you'll get more work done.

Second, you need a surface—a desk or a table—to write on. Writing on a book balanced in your lap almost guarantees sloppy penmanship; you may find you can't even read your own notes! Also, writing this way is tiring, because your arm is held in an awkward position.

Third, your homework materials need to be available while you study. Pencils and pens, scratch paper and good paper, as well as your textbooks and assignments, are all important—without them it's hard to do your work! In addition, you may need special equipment. If you're working on geometry, for example, don't leave your protractor and compass at school.

Is your regular study space also used by other members of your family—for eating or TV watching or whatever? If it is, you should have an easy method of moving your things out of the way when you're finished studying for the day. Try using a sturdy cardboard box that's big enough to hold all your equipment. You can keep the box under your bed and then you'll always know where to find it.

COMPUTERS

If you're lucky enough to have your own computer at home, you probably already have it set up in your study space. But if you share a computer with other members of the family, then you all have to have access to it. A shared computer means shared responsibility. It means making some rules you all agree on and sticking to them.

Perhaps you and your family have already decided on computer-sharing rules that work for all of you. But if not, now is the time to have a family meeting to discuss this issue. If you share computer time at school, you'll already have some helpful ideas on what to do and what not to do. Explaining these school rules to your family can be a good way to begin your family meeting.

Here are some things you need to discuss when you talk about rules for sharing a computer:

Access time. What time of day does each person want to use the computer? Maybe it will turn out that everyone prefers to use it at different times. Then there's no problem. But often there are conflicts about access time. Suppose you and your sister both want to use the computer most nights right after dinner. You might agree to alternate; for one week you'll use it after dinner and your sister will use it before dinner, and the next week you'll switch. Whatever compromise you reach, write it down and post it near the computer so everyone knows whose turn it is.

Computer file maintenance and use. Computers do sometimes crash. Computer files do get corrupted. These are sad facts of life in the computer age. It won't do any good to yell at your little brother if he loads in a program he got from a friend and a virus hidden in the program eats up all the files on the hard drive. It won't restore that school report you worked so long on but didn't save on a backup disk or drive!

There are, of course, safety measures everyone should take when using a computer. Make backups of your hard drive and of your own files often. Run your virus-checking program and keep it updated to control new viruses. Be cautious about loading programs that don't come shrink-wrapped from the factory and files that come over the Internet or attached to e-mail. Run hard disk scanning and organizing programs frequently. Install surge protectors and don't use your computer during violent lightning storms.

But even if you follow all these sensible safety precautions, it's still possible for your computer simply to crash. So be sure you make a separate backup of your own work every time before you end a computer session. It's sort of like brushing your teeth before you go to bed every night—once you've established the habit, it will feel like second nature to do it. And when the inevitable happens and the computer crashes, you can feel happy that at least your own material is saved.

Privacy. In some homes, the computer is divided into password-protected sections so that no one can accidentally open someone else's file and change something in it. Other families don't go to the trouble of password protection, but it's often a good idea for each person who uses the computer to have an area of hard disk space that's exclusively for his or her own use. Maybe you'll each have a directory with your name on it and you'll store all your files in that directory. Still, e-mail will probably be accessible to everyone who uses the computer, so keep that in mind when sending or receiving e-mail messages.

EXTRAS

There are lots of extras that are not strictly necessary for your study space but might be nice to have. Perhaps you already own a dictionary. This reference book is probably the most useful one for any student. For one thing, you can use it to check the correct spelling of a word. If you have a spelling checker on your computer, you may decide to use this program instead of a dictionary to see if you've spelled all the words in your report correctly. Remember, though, as long as you spell it correctly, your computer won't know if you use the *wrong* word ("their" instead of "there," for instance). So even if you use your spelling checker faithfully, you need to read over your work to make sure errors haven't crept in.

A dictionary is helpful in ways besides spelling. It can tell you exactly what a word means. It gives examples of how a specific word can be used in a sentence. And it lists synonyms (words with the same or similar meaning) for the word you're looking up.

Another handy reference tool is an atlas. The very large ones you see in libraries are quite expensive, but a smaller version in paperback is great to have. In addition to maps of countries and continents, it may give information about population, natural resources, climate, national and state flags, and so on.

If you can put up a bulletin board in your study space, you'll find it very convenient. Where else can you tack up that list of people who are working on the science project with you and what each of them is supposed to be doing? The great thing about a bulletin board is that what's pinned on it doesn't have to stay there forever—when you're finished with something, you can take it down and throw it away.

SETTING THE MOOD

Are you the type who likes to have the radio going in the background while you're doing your homework? Or do you prefer peace and quiet? Experts who study how people learn are convinced that there are different types of study habits. It appears that some students can concentrate best when there are no noises at all to distract them. Others, however, seem to need a steady flow of background sound to help them think. It may be that music on the radio blocks out other sounds, such as traffic noises or people calling to one another.

It's not hard to experiment to figure out which type you are. Try studying both ways and see what works best for you. Don't use this as an excuse to listen to your favorite DJ instead of studying! But if you really do get more done with the radio burbling quietly nearby, point this out to your mom the next time she tells you to "turn it off so you can concentrate." She may need some convincing if she's the type who prefers peace and quiet—it's up to you to prove your point by getting terrific grades on your homework.

Watching television while you study is another

matter, though. You need to have your eyes on your work and not on the flickering screen. And it's hard to keep yourself from getting caught up in a show that's on. If you do get drawn into the show, you'll find that you can hardly remember a thing from the chapter you thought you were reading.

It's interesting to see some of the other differences in the ways people like to study. Some find it best to sit in a straight-backed chair at a table or desk to read—they find they learn more this way. But others prefer to lounge on a bed or curl up in an armchair while reading a chapter or two. Such people may change position often, and it's possible that moving around helps them concentrate.

No one really knows why these variations in study patterns exist. But finding out how you work best is one step on the way to being school smart.

KEEP CLUTTER UNDER CONTROL

Here's another difference among people. Are you the type who puts every CD, cassette tape, or baseball card away in its own special spot every time? Or do you find yourself rooting around on the closet floor for the one comic book or computer game you're sure must be there somewhere?

Super-organized people are really lucky. They don't have to work at keeping their things neat and ready whenever they're needed, and this can be a big asset in handling schoolwork. But what about the rest of us, who may seem totally disorganized?

Don't let this worry you too much. Keep in mind that what looks like a mess to someone else may be a perfectly okay system of organization for you. It's not necessary to have everything you own filed in special folders and arranged in alphabetical order. You just have to be able to find the things you need when you need them.

One easy way to keep track of all your stuff is to stash it in cardboard boxes. Here's how to do it:

Clear off a large section of the floor and begin making piles of various things. Homework that's been handed back but should be kept for review goes in one pile. Materials for a research project or paper go in another pile. Bits of paper you can't bear to throw out (last year's birthday cards, the flyer from the amusement park you went to this summer, a photo from a magazine) are collected in a third pile. You get the idea. And of course, some things can go directly into the wastebasket.

Now look for boxes the right size for these various things you want to keep. For small items (like CDs, postcards, and the little oddments that accumulate on top of your dresser), shoe boxes are perfect. For papers, try to find a box that file folders came in or a shirt-size box from a department store. A local store may have extra boxes to give away if you ask. And of course, you can buy boxes at most office supply stores or at a place that specializes in wrapping and mailing packages.

Once everything is neatly sorted and boxed, it's a good idea to label each box. That way you'll remember what goes where, and you'll be reminded when you see the label that that's the box for your homework papers or basketball schedules or whatever.

You'll want to keep your boxes where you can get at them easily. Stacking them on a bookshelf is great. But if you don't have an empty shelf, think about other spaces that would work. What about the floor of your closet, next to your desk, or under your bed? Anyplace that is handy to reach will work fine.

GET THE GOOD OUT OF IT!

Now that you've put your study space together the way you want it, why not go ahead and use it?

There you are at your desk with your pencils in a Mickey Mouse mug from Disneyland, your papers gathered close at hand, and your reading light turned on. Sitting in the spot you've created for schoolwork definitely puts you more in the mood to do it. Now you're ready to tackle anything.

CHAPTER 3

ORGANIZING YOUR TIME

MAYBE YOU FEEL AS IF YOUR time is already a lot more organized than you'd like. You've got to go to school every morning, then get to your piano lesson or baseball practice, be home in time to do your chores before dinner, and still have your homework done before you can watch TV. Sometimes it seems as if there isn't time to do everything, and people are always telling you to hurry and not be late.

Even if you manage to get everything done, you may wish you had more time to play, to read a book or watch TV, or just to lie around and stare into space.

Most people feel this way. But if you

figure out how to use your time more efficiently, you will find you have more time to spend on things you enjoy.

How can you do this?

One method that works well for lots of people is to use a time chart for a couple of weeks. The idea is to learn how you really spend your time. You make a chart for the coming week and write down everything you plan to do and when you plan to do it. Then, at the end of each day, you fill in an identical chart with the things you actually did.

Comparing the two charts will tell you a lot about how you use your time. It will let you see how your time slips away without your noticing it. And when you know what's really happening each day, you'll be able to think of ways to get better organized.

Planning your time will take some effort. But you'll be amazed at how helpful the charts can be in just a short while.

HOW TO MAKE A TIME CHART

Your time chart will cover one whole week. To make the chart, you need two pieces of plain unlined 8½-x-11-inch paper, such as regular copier paper. (You can make your chart on a computer, but it's probably easier to do by hand.) Look at the sample on pages 22–23 and make yours the same way. Naturally, when you fill in the hours down the left side, you'll use your own schedule. If you get up at 6:00 A.M.—instead of 7:00 A.M., as in the sample—your time chart should start at six.

You will be taping these two papers together to make one complete chart, and you need two charts for each week. So before you start taping, make several copies of each half of the chart on a copying machine (it's much easier than doing it by hand!). You can use a coin-operated machine at the local copy shop or stationery store.

LET'S LOOK AT YOUR WEEK

When you've taped one chart together, you're ready to fill in all the things you know you'll be doing in the next week. It's easiest to start with all the things you do every week, like music lessons. The example on pages 26–27 shows one student's week.

Use a colored pencil to outline the block of time you spend in school. Then enter your regular plans in the correct boxes, or make half boxes for half-hour items. And don't forget religious services or dinner at your grandparents' house, if those are things you do every week.

	Monday	Tuesday	Wednesday
7:00 A.M.			
8:00			
9:00			
10:00			
11:00			
12:00 P.M.			
1:00			
2:00			
3:00			
4:00			
5:00			
6:00			
7:00			
8:00			

Thursday	Friday	Saturday	Sunday

In the example, Michael Jones wrote in these items: band practice (Tuesday morning, 8:30–9:00); music lesson (Friday afternoon, 4:00–5:00); Photography Club (Thursday lunchtime, 12:00–12:30); soccer practice (Tuesday and Thursday afternoons, 4:30–5:30); church (Sunday morning, 10:00); dinner at Grandma's house (Sunday evening, 6:00).

Now think over your own coming week and see if there are any unusual events to write down. You can see that Michael filled in several boxes with events like soccer games and birthday parties. When you've figured out what special plans you have for the week, enter them all on your time chart.

It's a good idea to write down any tests or quizzes you know are coming up this week. You'll want to plan extra time to study for them. As you can see, Michael has a spelling test on Wednesday at 1:30 and a science quiz Friday morning at 10:00. And the outline for his term paper is due a week from Monday, so he needs to allow time to work on it.

Once you've filled in everything you can think of, sit back and take a look at your week. It's probably pretty busy. And you haven't even added in time for getting up and having breakfast, going to school and back, feeding your pets, and talking on the phone to your friends.

MAKE A PLAN!

The best plan for you depends on your own schedule, and it won't be exactly the same as anyone else's. But let's take a look at Michael's time chart and see what might work well for him. He gets home from school by 3:30 every afternoon. That gives him a lot of time on Monday and Wednesday afternoons for homework and chores.

On Tuesday and Thursday afternoons, however, Michael has to be at soccer practice by 4:30. It will probably take him about twenty minutes to change into his shorts and team T-shirt and get to the practice field. That leaves him forty minutes of free time. How could he use it best? Perhaps that's long enough to do a spelling review or to finish most of his math assignment. On the other hand, it might be better for Michael to use that forty minutes to walk the dog and practice his music.

But wait a minute! This Tuesday he doesn't have that forty minutes before soccer practice— he'll be on the way home from the dentist's office. And besides, he has a big spelling test on

Michael's Planned Week	Monday	Tuesday	Wednesday
7:00 A.M.			
8:00		band practice	
9:00			
10:00			
11:00			
12:00 P.M.			
1:00			spelling tes
2:00			
3:00	walk dog	dentist	walk dog
4:00	music practice		music practi
	math & language	soccer	photograph
5:00	homework	practice	
		walk dog	
6:00	dinner	dinner	dinner
7:00		spelling & math homework	science & ma homework
8:00	TV	music practice	language home

Thursday	Friday	Saturday	Sunday
		at Jim's	
	science quiz	soccer game	church
otography Club		work on term paper	
			music practice
			walk dog
			movie
walk dog	walk dog		research at library
soccer	music lesson	birthday party	
practice	photography		
dinner	dinner & sleepover at Jim's	walk dog	dinner at Grandma's
		music practice	
h homework & er homework		TV	
for science quiz		TV	

Wednesday that he wants to study for. How would you solve a similar problem? Maybe Michael will be able to squeeze in some homework time during lunch on Tuesday, or he could get up extra early Wednesday morning.

Like Michael, you may find it hard to fit in all your activities, but it's also fun to arrange your schedule so it makes more sense. When you've filled in your own time chart for the coming week, pin it up on the bulletin board or your door so you can see what you're supposed to be doing each day.

HOW IS YOUR PLAN WORKING?

Now you get to do the most interesting part of the time chart. Save yourself five or ten minutes at the end of each day and fill out another copy of your time chart with the things you *really* did that day. You might be amazed at how different your two charts look by the end of the week!

Be as honest as you can when you write down what you actually spent your time on. No one is going to see this schedule but you, and you won't be graded on it. On pages 32–33 you can see what Michael did during the week, and you can compare it to what he had planned to do.

When you compare your plan with what you

ended up doing, you may find places where they don't match up at all. Don't get upset about this—most people plan to do more than is humanly possible. But by comparing the two charts, you can learn a lot about your study habits. You may see how to use your time in a way that works better for you.

MAKE A BETTER PLAN!

What are some of the things you might learn from your time charts? Perhaps you discovered that your homework took more time than you had allowed for it. What went wrong?

It may be, of course, that you simply didn't realize that your math or whatever takes forty-five minutes to complete, not just half an hour. Now that you know, you'll be able to allot enough time next week.

Or maybe you scheduled your day too tightly. Did you forget to allow time for changing your clothes after a ball game, or other "in-between" things like getting from one place to another? It's surprising to find out how much time gets eaten up that way.

Perhaps you planned to work for three hours in a row, but you found you just couldn't do it. This shouldn't make you feel bad—most people can't work for a long stretch of time without taking a break. In fact, some people do best if they work for a short period—twenty minutes or so—and then stop for a while. If you like to work this way, why not plan to walk the dog during your break? The exercise will be good for both of you, and you can probably settle down to another successful work period afterward.

Did you schedule your studying at the wrong time of day for you? That's what Michael did. If you look at his charts, you'll see that he planned to study a lot in the evenings after dinner. But he didn't actually get much done then. However, he did end up studying in the mornings before school, and it may be that that's the best time for him.

There really are "morning people" and "evening people." If you wake up every morning before the alarm goes off and you're full of energy from that moment on, why not try doing some of your homework or reviewing then? You might find it goes faster and you do it better than if you wait until after dinner, when your brain feels tired.

Some people get too nervous if they leave their homework until the morning it's due. And other people don't do their best work early in the day.

But Michael Jones found that he got a lot accomplished in the mornings before school, and he also found that he *didn't* get nearly as much done after dinner as he had planned. If this is your pattern, too, you can adjust your plan for the next week.

Another thing your time charts can show you is how much time you spend fooling around. Michael had looked forward to the movie on Sunday. But when that time rolled around, he hadn't done any of the work for his term paper, so he had to cancel. Looking over his week, you can see how it happened.

Everyone needs some time for just fooling around—no one can or should plan to work all the time. But maybe you can adjust your schedule so you'll get the most good out of your free time. For example, Michael might decide that he's been goofing off too much in the afternoons. Maybe instead of taking a half hour to walk the dog and a half hour to have a snack, he could eat an apple while he walks the dog—then he'd be able to get down to studying at 4:00. And it worked well to practice his music right after dinner, so maybe he'll plan it that way for next week. Then he'll have time for a movie over the weekend.

The whole point of finding out what you actually

Michael's Actual Week	Monday	Tuesday	Wednesday
7:00 A.M.			
8:00		band practice	spelling review
9:00			
10:00			
11:00			
12:00 P.M.			
1:00			spelling test
2:00			
3:00			
3:00	snack	dentist	snack
4:00	talk to Jim	change & go to field	photography
4:00	walk dog	soccer	music practice
5:00	math homework	practice	walk dog
5:00	math homework	walk home & change	talk on phone
6:00	dinner	dinner	dinner
7:00	music practice	music practice	science homework
7:00	language homework	math	fool around
8:00	TV	spelling	language
8:00	TV	talk on phone	?

hursday	Friday	Saturday	Sunday
		at Jim's	
math	math homework		
omework	science review		
	science quiz	soccer game	church
			lunch
ography Club		fool around	library—work on term paper
		lunch	
		buy present	walk dog
		walk dog	work on term paper
walk dog	snack	shower & change	
ge & go to field	music lesson	birthday party	photography
soccer			
practice	walk dog		music practice
ome & change	fool around		
dinner	sleepover at Jim's	walk home	dinner at Grandma's
		music practice	
or science quiz		TV	TV
on phone		TV	

do every hour for a whole week is to learn what works and doesn't work for you. With this in mind, you can plan your time according to your personal "internal clock" instead of trying to force yourself to fit someone else's pattern.

Try keeping time charts for yourself for two or three weeks. By then you'll have learned a lot about your own study habits. You'll probably find you're beginning to get more work done in less time. Later on, if you start to feel disorganized, you can keep weekly charts again until you get back on track.

LOOKING AT THE BIG PICTURE

Another terrific tool to help keep your time organized is a large monthly calendar. Try to find the kind that is used as a desk blotter; these usually measure at least 1½ x 2 feet. They are made like a pad of paper, and you tear off each month when it is finished. There is a large square for each day, so it's easy to write down the things you need to remember.

Hang the calendar on the wall or lay it flat on your desk—just make sure to keep it somewhere handy so you'll look at it every day.

The idea is to enter all the important events

that are coming up in the next month. The due date for a term paper, the days when tests will be given, and the times of parties or athletic events can all be noted on this big calendar. If you have a part-time job, like baby-sitting or yard work, be sure to make a note of those times too. Then you'll be able to look ahead and get an idea of how to arrange your study time and your social time.

If you look around at the people you know, you'll notice that most busy adults keep a monthly calendar. It lets them know what's coming up and helps them feel in control of their lives. It can do the same thing for you! Making notes of what's going to happen and glancing at them every day or two will keep you from being surprised by that midterm test and will remind you to get going on the science project or term paper you have to turn in next month.

As you get in the habit of using a calendar to keep track of your life, jotting down notes of future events will become almost automatic. You'll feel that you really know what you're doing and you'll be amazed at how much you accomplish. Besides, it's fun to decide how to use all that extra time you've saved!

CHAPTER 4

DIFFERENT WAYS OF LEARNING

THERE ARE MANY DIFFERENT WAYS to learn things, and most of these ways are used in school. Does this surprise you? Think about it. In school you learn by reading words in books; by looking at, or "reading," picture languages like maps, graphs, and charts; by listening to and watching films and videotapes; by listening to teachers talk; by making displays or dioramas; by typing on a computer keyboard and reading what appears on the screen; by doing experiments that demonstrate ideas; by writing down spelling words and math calculations; by writing essays that explain your ideas; and by memorizing a poem or a list of words in another language. You can probably think of other ways you learn.

People who study education have done research about different learning styles. It seems that there are three main ways that people learn things: by seeing (which includes reading), by hearing, and by touching or working with things.

HOW DO YOU LEARN BEST?

Most people use all their senses to learn things, and they don't learn in only one way. But some students find that they learn better in one way than in others. It can be very helpful to know which learning styles work best for you.

Perhaps you already know something about the way you learn. Do you remember things best if you hear them explained out loud in words? Or do you do better if you read those things in a book? Some people feel they really know something only if they write it down themselves.

Think about how you learn new spelling words. Are you the type of student who memorizes the way words are spelled by looking at them? Or do you remember the way the letters are arranged by spelling the words out loud? Or perhaps the easiest way for you to be sure you are ready for a spelling test is to write each new word down a couple of times. And it's possible that you use two or even all three of these ways of learning.

TRICKS FOR BETTER READING

Reading is perhaps the most important skill for doing well in school. It seems that you are always reading, not only for language arts but also for social studies, science, and even math.

Sometimes when you're faced with studying a big section of text, you may feel as though you can't remember a thing you read. But there are tricks for getting the most out of the pages you are supposed to read and understand.

LOOK BEFORE YOU LEAP!

Many of the books you read for school have lots of headings and other guideposts to learning. Chapter titles and subtitles, section summaries, questions to think about, marginal notes, and captions for pictures, graphs, and maps are all helpful tools for you to use.

Before you begin your actual reading assignment, take time to page through your book and look at titles, headings, and summaries. Many chapters have introductions, and these are worth reading. An introduction tells you in short form what you are about to learn when you read that chapter.

The people who write textbooks want to help you learn. Take advantage of the clues they provide about the material you are going to read. One of these clues is the kind of type used in the headings and subheadings. The most important topics usually have headings in larger type or in darker type, called **boldface.** Reading them will let you know what the chapter is about.

Textbooks often have a list of questions at the beginning or end of each chapter. Take a look at the questions before you read the chapter. Reading them out loud to yourself might help fix them in your mind. The questions will give you an idea of what kinds of information you will be expected to know after you've finished reading the material. Keep these questions in mind as you read, and the answers will probably leap right off the page at you!

READ IT YOUR WAY

Reading for a school subject is not quite the same as reading a novel for fun. After reading a class assignment, you are expected to remember the information and to be able to join in a class discussion. Sometimes it's hard to keep all those facts and ideas in your head, but there are ways to make it easier. Why not use your knowledge of learning styles to come up with a method that works well for you?

THE EYES HAVE IT

If you learn best by reading, a good way to make sure you understand a chapter is to go back over the headings and questions. As you read each heading and subheading, think about what information that section contains. Then, when you reread the questions, see if you can give a good answer to each one. You may find that you remember what part of the chapter the answer comes from; you may even "see" the words on the page in your mind's eye.

LET'S HEAR IT

If you learn best by listening, a tape recorder is a handy tool. Try reading the entire chapter onto the tape and then listening to it. This way you hear it twice. Or you might find that it's just as effective to take taped notes as you read. After reading each short section, turn on the tape recorder, read the section heading out loud, and then give a short verbal summary of what the section contains.

Once you've read the whole assignment, read the questions from the book onto your tape and give an answer to each in your own words. Be sure to look back through the chapter to check any facts you're not sure of.

Every time you listen to your tape, it's like reading the information all over again, so these tapes will be very helpful when you are reviewing for a test. Just be sure to label each tape clearly with the book and chapter titles as well as the date. Then you can easily find the parts you need to review. When you've taken your final test in that class, you can erase the tape and use it for another subject.

REACH OUT AND TOUCH IT

Maybe you have discovered you learn best through movement and your sense of touch. In that case, you'll want to write down notes as you read through your material. The act of picking up a pencil and shaping the words helps many people remember facts and ideas. (Typing on a computer does not seem to have the same effect of "imprinting" the words in your mind as you put them down. But if you type your notes, you'll still have the notes to read through later—you just won't have taken advantage of this style of learning.)

Keep some paper and a pencil nearby while you read. Write the headings as you come to them, and when you've read that section, jot down a brief summary of the main ideas. You don't have to be super-neat, since these notes won't be turned in. But be sure you can read what you've written.

When you've finished, you will have an outline of the material contained in that chapter. Your notes will be arranged in the order the author used in writing. But you may find it helpful to arrange the words and phrases in a different pattern. On another sheet of paper you could write down a main idea and draw a circle around it. Then you could connect other related facts and ideas to it with lines and arrows.

However you arrange the information from the chapter, every time you write it down you help your mind remember it.

MAKE YOUR OWN LEARNING TOOLS

You can take advantage of many learning methods by making and using flash cards. These cards are a great way to learn lists of information like vocabulary words and their definitions, math facts, or words in a foreign language.

Flash cards are easy to make out of 3-x-5-inch index cards. Write the question on one side and the answer on the other. For example, for a Spanish vocabulary card, the front would say "azul" and the back would say "blue."

Once you have a set of cards, you can use them in various ways. Go through them by yourself, one by one, checking the backs to make sure your answers are right. Set aside the ones you didn't know right away to go through a second time.

Or use the flash cards with a friend. As your friend holds up the cards, one at a time, you call out each answer. (Your friend can see the correct answers on the backs of the cards.) Take turns until you both know the material. And don't forget that you can flip the cards over and ask the questions the other way around.

For some students, the very act of writing out the information may be the most helpful part of using flash cards. But for others, the repetition of saying the answers out loud or seeing the correct information flashed in front of their eyes will be the best memory aid.

You can probably think of many other ways to

use the different methods of learning. Have you ever heard of a mnemonic device? It's a memory aid, usually a word or phrase that helps you remember a list or sequence. Here's a famous example: "Every good boy does fine." The first letters of these words are E G B D F, the notes of the lines in the treble clef in music. And who is ROY G. BIV? This name spells out the initials of the colors of the spectrum—red, orange, yellow, green, blue, indigo, and violet. You can make up your own mnemonic devices for other lists. What about a phrase to help you remember the order of the planets in our solar system?

Once you get started, you'll think up lots of creative ways to learn. You might make a map that's really a puzzle to help you remember where all the states are. Or you could create a skit using the foreign language vocabulary you're supposed to learn. You could even make a board game to help you in one of your classes. Paint a piece of cardboard with a path for the markers to follow. Then make up a bunch of question cards—you could use questions about history facts, for example. When a player lands on a question square, he or she has to draw a card and answer the question correctly in order to move ahead. Let your imagination roam free, and you'll no doubt come up with lots of other creative learning tools.

No matter what you think your learning style is, it's a good idea to try a few different ones. Many people learn best using a combination of styles. And your style may change as you get older. So use a variety of learning methods to be truly school smart.

CHAPTER 5

HANDLING HOMEWORK

EVEN THOUGH YOU DON'T DO IT at school, homework is an important part of your schoolwork. It allows you to practice the things you learn in class—a set of math problems, for instance, might use the math ideas the teacher presented that day.

Homework also gives you a chance to do work that takes a lot of time. For example, you might read a chapter in your textbook for homework and then discuss it the next day in class. If you had to read it in school in addition to discussing it, you wouldn't be able to get as much done.

Preparing for tests is also a kind of homework. When you read over the chapters you'll be tested on or review the spelling words from the last few weeks, you may not think of it as homework. But in fact it is schoolwork that you are doing at home, even though your teacher may not have assigned it.

Other kinds of homework may be long-term projects. You might be asked to do research and write a paper that is due six weeks from now. Of course, you can't do the whole project the night before it's due. It's up to you to plan your time and get each stage of this kind of homework done so your project will be ready when it should be.

TOOLS FOR SCHOOL

In addition to the pencils and pens you need for class, a very important tool for school is a way of keeping your assignments and homework together and easy to find. How many times have you called a friend in a panic because you didn't know what the homework was? Of course you wrote it down, but later you couldn't find the paper you wrote it on.

One way to make sure you always have the assignment is to write it in your notebook for that class. Do you keep your notes from science or social studies class in a spiral-bound or loose-leaf notebook? Use that same notebook for each day's homework assignment as well.

The problem with using the small notebooks sold as assignment pads is that they can easily become separated from the rest of your books. By keeping all of the information for one class together—homework *and* class notes—you make it a lot easier for yourself. You can look over what's happened in class so far and review all the work you've done since the beginning of the year.

Both spiral-bound and loose-leaf notebooks come with pocket folders included. These are great for keeping all your handouts (the poem you have to read tonight, the math problems that are due tomorrow, the map of major rivers to be learned for social studies) collected and available. You can't do your homework if you don't have the sheet it's written on. And loose papers always fall out of notebooks at the worst possible times—this seems to be a law of nature! A notebook with pockets will be a big help. If your bound notebook doesn't have a pocket, make one by gluing a cut-down manila envelope to the inside front or back cover.

It's also hard to do your homework if you haven't written down the assignment correctly.

Listen carefully when your teacher tells you what to do for the next day. Sometimes those directions will be different from the ones in the textbook. Maybe the book says you should give only "true" or "false" as answers to the questions at the end of the chapter—but your teacher wants everyone to write whole sentences explaining the answers as well. This is the kind of thing it's important to pay attention to.

HELPFUL HINTS FOR HOMEWORK

Perhaps your teacher has already given you some suggestions for studying more effectively. Or maybe you've picked up an idea or two from watching how your friends do their homework. Here are some ways of dealing with your homework that you may not have thought of before.

BREAKING UP THE JOB

When you have a large assignment to complete, separate it into smaller pieces. The idea of reading a long chapter of difficult science material may seem overwhelming to you. But if you break up the job into manageable segments, you'll feel more able to get started. Decide to read only the first one or two subsections; that will be the end of the job for now. Later—maybe after dinner or the next morning—you can read the next two subsections, and so on until the whole chapter is finished. Naturally, this works only if you have enough time to split up the assignment over a couple of days.

One reason this method works is that it makes the job look easier. After all, just about anyone can read two short subsections of a chapter. If you focus on one piece at a time, you are more likely to get started.

This method also helps by giving you enough time between segments to make sure you understand the material. You'll be able to think over the shorter part that you've finished before moving on to another section. Even quite difficult assignments become easier to grasp when you approach them like this.

Breaking up a job into smaller sections works for assignments other than reading. Think of your five-page term paper and all the research and writing it will require. You can separate the work into three major chunks: doing the research, making the outline, and writing the paper itself. Divide up the time you have until the paper is due and enter the dates you plan to finish each work segment on your calendar. Attacking this kind of project in smaller bits will help get the job done on time.

GIVE YOURSELF A TREAT

Why not give yourself a reward when you finish a hard assignment? Knowing that a treat is awaiting you often makes you more eager to get the job done. You might promise yourself a half hour of playing ball or watching TV. Or maybe you'll save the next chapter of that exciting novel or a telephone chat with a friend until after you've done your math homework.

Rewards actually work, and you know best what will make you get busy. Just be sure that the treat you promise yourself isn't more than the job deserves. Watching TV for two hours is way too big a reward for completing a fifteen-minute spelling review. And don't get in the habit of using sweets or junk food to treat yourself—they're not good for either your brain or your body.

USE A TIMER

Do you try to do all of your math homework at one sitting and find that your brain is bogging down before you're finished? Maybe you'd be better off with a timer. Some people find that they concentrate best for a short period of time, like half an hour.

Why not see if it works for you? Set a timer for half an hour and then settle down with whatever assignment you plan to work on. When the timer goes off, stop what you are doing and mark your place. Now take a five-minute break to stretch and clear your mind before going back to work. You may find that this short pause renews your energy and enthusiasm so that you can work efficiently for another half hour.

Another way to do timed homework is to change to another kind of assignment after your five-minute break. If you've been doing math problems, start on your reading for social studies for the next half hour. And you might even want to move on to review for your science quiz for a third half hour before returning to the math. Mixing the types of work and fields of study often will help your mind stay alert.

At first glance, this way of studying may sound confusing. But many students find that it is an effective method of staying on top of their homework. It is especially useful in dealing with jobs that really have no end, like studying foreign language vocabulary or reviewing for a test. You could keep working on either one of these all night. Using a timer lets you know when you've done enough, at least for now.

USE A LIST

Are you someone who takes a lot of pleasure in finishing something and crossing it off your list? If so, using a timer method to do your homework might make you want to tear out your hair.

For some students, completing an assignment feels like a reward all by itself. If you are one of these people, make a list of your homework each day so that you can keep track of what has to be done. Just make sure that you don't load your list up so much that there is no possibility of doing it all. And it's still a good idea to take a break from time to time. When you find yourself slowing down or feeling drowsy, jog around the block or play on the floor with the cat for a change of pace.

What about open-ended jobs? If the idea of using a timer to decide how long to review for a quiz or study your vocabulary words doesn't appeal to you, here are some other possibilities. You can decide in advance how many times you will go through your list of definitions or whatever.

When you've done it as many times as you've decided on, that job is finished. Cross it off your list and move on to the next assignment.

Another way to handle open-ended work is to test yourself. Let's say you are memorizing the names of U.S. presidents and the dates they held office. Go over the information a number of times until you feel you know it, and then try to write the names and dates on a blank piece of paper. If you can do it with no more than one or two mistakes, you're ready for the test in class.

HARD STUFF OR EASY STUFF FIRST?

Whatever works best for you is the right answer to this question. Some people believe that the best way to study is to work on a hard subject first. Then working on an easier subject afterward is sort of like a reward. These people hate knowing that the hard stuff is sitting there waiting for them. They like to get it over with first.

Other people feel strongly that beginning with a topic that's easy for them is a better way to work. It puts them in the studying mood and makes them feel ready to tackle harder subjects. Besides, they like being able to cross one assignment off their lists, even if it's something easy.

You might want to try each of these methods and see if one works better for you. Maybe you'll be surprised at how much more you accomplish.

WORKING ALONE OR WORKING WITH OTHERS

Whether you decide to work on a particular project by yourself or with others often depends on the assignment. It also depends on the kind of person you are. Some students prefer wrestling with homework problems by themselves. They may be worried that others will think they're stupid if they don't catch on to everything right away. Or students may find they're tempted to chat instead of work when they do homework with friends.

Others don't feel comfortable facing a pile of work all alone. They can get going on their assignments better if there are other people around. And sometimes being in a situation where a number of people are working helps these students stay focused.

Maybe you already know from experience that you and your best friend don't do much homework when you're together. Even though you both plan to work, you end up just fooling around. But perhaps when you try to work by yourself, you seem to spend all your time sharpening your pencils or staring into space. Why not try studying in the library? Everyone around you will also be working, but it's not a place where you can giggle and goof off.

Some projects really are best done alone. It's hard to imagine how you could share reading an assigned chapter or writing a term paper with someone else. On the other hand, studying a foreign language or math facts by using flash cards works very well with a friend.

LOOK IT OVER ONE MORE TIME

Some homework—such as reviewing for a quiz or reading a chapter in your textbook so that you are ready to discuss it the next day—does not have to be written. That is the kind of homework you carry to school with you in your head. But other homework is meant to be written out—your math problems, or your essay for language arts, or your report for social studies.

It's a good idea to look over written homework one last time before you put your studying away for the evening. Homework needs to be neat enough for the teacher to read easily. It doesn't have to be absolutely perfect, with no cross-outs, unless your teacher says so. But it should look as if you care enough to do a good job. Don't forget that your teacher has a number of homework assignments to grade, and it's always more pleasant to look at work that is neatly done.

Check your homework for mistakes before taking it to school to turn in. If you are careful to line up the columns in your math problems, you will make fewer errors. Look up the spelling of words you're not sure of so that they are correct. And even if you use your computer's spelling checker, be sure to reread your paper carefully—if you typed "has" instead of "as," the error will pass unnoticed by your computer. If you're not using a computer, try reading your homework paper backward; spelling errors are more likely to jump out at you.

It's a good idea to gather up all your homework and school books before you go to bed at night so that they will all be in one place in the morning. It's easy to forget an important piece of homework in the morning when you are rushing to get to school on time.

Knowing that you've done all your homework to

the best of your ability gives you a good feeling as you start your day. You'll be ready to participate in class discussions with enthusiasm, and if you have a test, you'll be able to tackle it with confidence.

CHAPTER 6

GETTING A HEAD START ON TESTS

WHEN YOUR TEACHER ANNOUNCES that a test is coming up, how do you feel? Do you look at tests as exciting challenges, or does the thought of one send you into a panic?

Many students are nervous about taking tests. Sometimes it's because they're afraid they don't completely understand the material or they haven't studied it enough. But even students who feel sure they know the stuff they'll be tested on often get worried and upset when a test looms on the horizon.

WHAT'S A TEST FOR ANYWAY?

You've probably asked yourself this question many times, especially if taking tests is one of your least favorite things to do. Is this just another way for the school people to drive you crazy? The answer is no. A test is a way of measuring how much of the class material you have learned. By giving the same test to the entire class, your teacher can find out how well each of you understands the material being covered.

You might even think of the test you take in class as a test for the teacher as well. Students' test scores not only tell how the students have done but also give a good idea of how well the teacher has taught the material.

But teachers don't get grades based on test results; you do. And to do your best on a test, it pays to be prepared.

PREPARING FOR TESTS

Did you realize that homework is partly a method of preparing you for tests? That means that if you've been doing your homework all along, you'll be in pretty good shape when test time rolls around. That's a big help, because what your parents and teachers tell you really is true: You can't learn a whole unit by trying to cram all the information into your head in one night. Doing homework as it is assigned gives you time to think through the material from class and see how it all goes together. If you've understood your homework assignments, you probably have a better grasp of the subject than you think.

Nevertheless, almost all students need to do some extra studying to prepare for tests. What's the best method of doing it? You could reread all the material, but that's often not necessary. If you have been doing well on your homework and have been able to understand the class discussion, here's one way to approach test preparation.

Page through the whole section of your textbook that the test will cover. Read the introduction, if there is one, to remind yourself of the main idea. Then move on, reading only the headings and subheadings. Turn each one into questions and think about how you would answer them. For instance, if a heading is "The French Explore the New World," you might ask yourself, "Who were the important French explorers? When did they come to the New World? What part of the New World did they explore?"

If you can answer these questions, go on to the next heading. If you're not sure, read this section of the text to remind yourself.

Perhaps you have notes that you took in class.

Now is the time to read them over, but don't simply skim through them. Stop and think about what questions your teacher asked during the class discussion. This helps you focus on the important points, and it might even give you an idea of what kind of questions will be on the test.

How else can you prepare for a test? Try looking through the homework papers and work sheets from this study unit. As you read them, you may remember more ideas or facts to fit into your overall understanding of the material.

Reviewing homework papers is especially useful when you're studying for a math test. You can try working two or three problems from each page of homework—be sure to cover up the answers as you work. If you find you have trouble with certain kinds of problems, you can practice doing a few more of them.

For spelling and foreign language vocabulary tests, use the lists of words that were handed out or get out your flash cards. Ask a friend or a family member to help you review. Put a pencil mark on the list beside any words you don't know, or set aside those flash cards to go over again.

When you use these review techniques, getting ready for a test takes less time. You'll feel confident that you've focused on the important material and that you're well prepared for the questions.

GET A HEAD START

One of the best ways you can help yourself do well on tests is to make sure that you feel rested and alert. You've probably heard a million times that you should get a good night's sleep before a test, and the reason you've heard it so often is that it's true! Staying up late to study for a test rarely helps. Your brain is unlikely to retain much so late at night, and the next day you'll be slowed down and exhausted just when you need to be your most energetic.

You'll probably gather up your school stuff and put it somewhere handy the night before so you can snatch it up as you leave for school. But did you ever think of deciding ahead of time what clothes you'll wear on test day? It may sound like a weird idea if you don't do it already, but why not give it a try?

It's important to wear comfortable clothes when you're taking a test. After all, you want to be able to concentrate on the test questions, not on the waistband that's too tight or the sweater that itches around your neck. But don't wear your oldest and grubbiest outfit. One of the things that helps most on test day is a feeling of confidence; wearing something you look good in makes you feel this way.

Many students are nervous on the morning of a big test. If that's what happens to you, looking good and having your stuff all ready to go will help you relax a little. Get up early enough so you don't have to rush. Being in your seat in plenty of time will help you get set to do your best. And don't forget to eat a good breakfast. Both your body and your brain need food.

USE YOUR HEAD

At last you're sitting at your desk—well prepared, rested, and ready to go. You're probably tempted to grab your pencil and plunge in. But wait! Here are a few tips that can be useful no matter what kind of test you are taking.

THINK AHEAD

First of all, glance through the whole test to see how long it is and what kinds of questions are in it. This preview gives you a chance to see what's coming; maybe there's an essay question at the end or a whole bunch of fill-in-the-blank sentences.

Looking over the test also lets you plan your time so you don't spend too long on any one section. For example, if you have half an hour for the whole test, you don't want to spend twenty-eight minutes on the multiple choice part and leave yourself only two minutes for an essay question. And don't forget that you'll want a few minutes at the end to go back and check your work. Try to allow this time so you can correct any careless mistakes before you hand in the test. A quick look through the whole thing before you get started is a good test-taking trick that can put you ahead of the game.

GET THE MESSAGE

Another useful idea is to read the test directions carefully before you pick up your pencil and begin marking your answers. This may seem obvious, but many students are so anxious to get going that they don't take time for this important step. Nothing makes you feel worse than to do poorly on a test you knew the answers to just because you didn't follow the instructions correctly. Take a couple of minutes at the start of each section of the test to think through what you're supposed to do. It will be time well spent.

START OFF EASY

Unless your teacher tells you otherwise, there's no law that says you have to answer the test questions in order. So why not do the easy ones first?

First of all, writing down the answers you're sure of is bound to make you more confident. Knowing you've already answered some questions correctly gives you the feeling that you're on your way, moving full speed ahead.

In addition, as you answer those easy questions, you'll be reminded of other facts that will help you answer the hard ones. This isn't so surprising—your test probably covers only one unit or topic, and all the information you've learned is related. So instead of letting your brain come to a halt when you're stumped by a difficult question, just keep going. Then, when you go back to that tough problem, the answer may well pop right into your mind.

Doing the easy questions first also means that at least the answers you're sure of will be written down. This is nice to know in case you didn't plan quite right and you run out of time.

MAKE YOUR ANSWERS CLEAR

Neatness on tests can make a big difference. Some students mistakenly believe that if they write sloppily enough, the teacher will think their unreadable scrawl actually is the right answer. But, in fact, answers a teacher can't read get marked wrong. So take care to make your work easily understandable. That way your correct answers will get full credit.

What if you see that you made a mistake in answering one of the questions? This happens to everyone from time to time. Of course you'll want to change it. Just be sure that your new answer can be read clearly. Either completely erase the original answer or totally cross it out. If you simply write one number or letter on top of the other, your teacher will have to be a mind reader to know which one you meant.

DON'T GIVE UP

Once you've written in all the answers you're pretty sure of, go back to the beginning of the test and look at the questions that had you stumped. Maybe by now you've come up with answers to some of them. But there might be a few that you still can't figure out. Unless your teacher has told you not to, go ahead and make a guess. After all, there's always a chance that you'll be right. And once you've read the tips on various kinds of questions in the next chapter of this book, your chances of guessing right will be even better.

CHAPTER 7

TACKLING TESTS

NATURALLY, THE BEST WAY TO DO well on tests is to study hard enough so that you can answer the test questions correctly. Tests are designed to measure how much of the subject you have learned. But even when you do know the material, some test questions can be difficult to answer. Don't despair—there are ways of figuring out how to deal with those tough questions.

TRUE-FALSE QUESTIONS

In a true-false question, you read a statement and have to decide whether it's true or not. Even if you're sure of your facts, be on the lookout for words like "never," "always," "every," and "none."

These are danger words that should make you stop and think carefully before marking your answer. A statement containing a danger word is usually false, because these words mean there are no exceptions. For example, is this statement true or false?

All kids love ice cream.

The statement is false. Maybe you don't know anyone who doesn't like ice cream, but somewhere in the world there's sure to be at least one kid who hates it. If the statement said "Most kids love ice cream," it would be true.

In the same way, be careful of statements that give causes or reasons. If it sounds as if it is the *only* reason for something, the statement is probably false. Here's an example:

When a dog barks, it is because he is angry.

This statement is clearly false. A dog might bark because he is happy, or lonely, or for some reason we don't even know about. You could turn this into a true statement by saying, "When a dog barks, it may be because he is angry."

Remember there are *some* statements that *are*

true even though they contain one of the danger words. You know that "All circles are round" is a true statement. So think each question through as you take a true-false test, and be certain that you know what each statement really means.

Here's one more tip from the experts who study how tests are made. They say that there are usually more true statements than false ones in a test. That means that if you have to guess, you're probably better off marking the statement "true."

MULTIPLE-CHOICE QUESTIONS

These are either incomplete statements followed by a number of possible endings or questions with a list of possible answers. You have to choose which ending or answer is correct.

Often you can pick out the right answer immediately. But if not, don't waste time searching for the one that's correct. Instead, narrow the field and get rid of the choices you know are wrong. How can you do this?

ANSWERS THAT ARE LIKELY TO BE WRONG

As in true-false questions, you can usually assume that an answer with a danger word is wrong. Words like "all," "none," "everybody," and "nobody" in an answer should make you think about eliminating that choice. What danger word answer can you eliminate from the example below?

The reason most Americans eat turkey on Thanksgiving is that
  a. everybody likes turkey.
  b. turkeys have carunculate heads.
  c. turkeys say "gobble, gobble."
  d. turkey is the traditional main dish.

If you decided *a* was wrong, you were right!

Now take a look at choice *b*. You probably don't know what "carunculate" means. (It refers to the wattles that hang down under a turkey's beak.) Even if you had been studying Thanksgiving and turkeys in school, it is unlikely that you've ever seen the word "carunculate." When you see a completely unfamiliar word or phrase, you can almost always get rid of that choice. Teachers don't expect students to know information that wasn't in the material they studied.

In this example, choice *b,* all by itself, is a true statement—turkeys *do* have heads with wattles on them. But this is not the reason most people eat turkey on Thanksgiving. So even though it's true, it's not the right answer and you can eliminate it.

Now that you've rejected two of the four choices, is there another one you can get rid of? It's a safe bet that a really ridiculous or jokey answer is not the right one. So choice *c* can't be correct. And that leaves you with answer *d*.

You probably knew the correct answer the moment you finished reading this question about turkey. It was pretty obvious that three of the choices were wrong. But they are good examples of the kinds of answers you might find in a multiple-choice test. Keep your eyes open for choices that contain danger words, words you've never run across in your studying, and silly suggestions. Once you've eliminated these possibilities, you may often find that you're left with only one answer—the right one.

In multiple-choice questions involving numbers, there's another trick you can try. Experts have found that the largest and smallest numbers are often choices you can eliminate. For some reason, people who make up tests tend to surround the correct answer with wrong answers that are higher and lower. Try this question and see how you do:

How many feet are in a mile?

    a. 528

    b. 5,280

    c. 52,800

    d. 528,000

If a question like this has you completely stumped, you can try eliminating the highest and lowest answers—in this case, *a* and *d*. Just getting rid of a couple of the possible choices makes it easier to think about the ones that are left. And often you'll recognize one of the remaining two possibilities as the right answer. Did you remember that *b* is the correct answer to this question?

ANSWERS THAT ARE LIKELY TO BE RIGHT

Just as there are ways to eliminate wrong answers for some questions, there are ways to pick out the correct answers for certain kinds of multiple-choice questions. One of these is to see if there are two similar-looking answers in your group of choices. If so, it is probable that one of them is correct. Once again, narrowing the possibilities down to two choices won't tell you which of those two is the right answer. But at least you've given yourself a better chance to make a correct guess. Take a look at the following question:

Which explorer is known for conquering
the Aztec people in Mexico?
    a. Joliet
    b. Hudson
    c. Cortés
    d. Coronado

Obviously the names Cortés and Coronado look
a lot alike. And once you've gotten that far, maybe
you'll remember that the man who conquered the
Aztecs was Cortés.

Another type of question to look for is one
where a choice is "all of the above." This, too,
tends to be a correct answer. And if you're pretty
sure that two of the other choices are correct,
you'll know you should pick "all of the above."
Take a look at this example:

Which of these foods is high in calcium?
    a. milk
    b. cheese
    c. broccoli
    d. all of the above

Let's say you know that both milk and cheese
have plenty of calcium, but you're not too sure
about broccoli. Don't waste time worrying about

the broccoli. Since you can only choose one answer, you have to take the one that includes both milk and cheese; answer *d* is correct.

DON'T EXPECT MAGIC

Keep in mind that tricks for choosing right answers won't work all the time. There are lots of questions that don't follow these patterns. And if these tricks were foolproof, everyone could get perfect test scores every time.

There's no substitute for studying, and there's nothing more satisfying than doing well on a test because you really understand the material you've worked hard to learn. But even if you are completely prepared for a test, you may feel nervous about it. And, like anyone else, you may run across a question you can't answer. These techniques will give you a way of getting started on tough questions.

FILL IN THE BLANKS

This is a very common kind of test question, and when you come across one, there's no way you can guess at the answer successfully. After all, you're not just taking a chance on one of two or one of four possibilities—you're coming up with a word on your own.

However, you can often find a clue by reading the whole sentence. Can you tell what kind of word is needed to complete it? If you can, you'll be more likely to figure out the correct fill-in answer. Try this one:

Columbus first sailed from _____ to the New World in the year _____.

It's pretty obvious that the second blank needs a date to complete it—in this case, 1492. Did you figure out that the first blank needs the name of a country? (The answer is Spain.) Most fill-in questions aren't quite this easy, but they do contain clues to the kind of word you should be looking for.

After you've filled in all the blanks, read each sentence over again to make sure your answer makes sense.

MATCHING LISTS

In this kind of question, there are two lists, and you have to match each item from one list with an item from the other. You either draw lines to connect the matching pairs or write the correct letter or number next to each item in one of the lists.

Looking at two lists of words or phrases can be

kind of confusing, even if you know all the material you're being tested on. Here's a good way to reduce your confusion. Start by looking at the top item on one of the lists; cover up the rest of that list with your hand or a piece of blank paper. Now you can concentrate on choosing the item from the other list that matches best with the word you're working on, and you won't get distracted by all the others.

Here's a sample to try:

1. reservation	a. built earthworks east of the Mississippi River
2. caribou	b. land set aside for Indians
3. Eskimos	c. home of the Shoshone
4. buffalo	d. food for Eskimos
5. Mound Builders	e. hunted on the Great Plains
6. Great Basin	f. last Indian group to come to North America

It's often easier to start with a definition and look through the other column for the word that's being defined. So take a look at item *a*. You can tell that the answer must be a group of people, not a place or a kind of animal. But is it "Eskimos" or "Mound Builders"? If you're not sure, the word

"Builders" gives you a clue that these people probably were the ones who "built" earthworks, so *a* matches with *5*.

Now look at *b*—this one is pretty easy, and you shouldn't have much trouble matching it with "reservation." And when you go on to *c*, the only place name on the first list is "Great Basin," so you can match up *c* with *6*. (If you hadn't already used "reservation," you might think it is the answer for "home of the Shoshone." But if you matched up *1* and *c*, you wouldn't have a definition for "reservation," so you can feel fairly sure that the way you have answered must be correct.)

When you've gotten this far, the rest is easy. The word that matches "food for Eskimos" has to be either "caribou" or "buffalo." But you probably remember that buffalo lived on the Great Plains, and caribou lived farther north in what is now Canada and Alaska, so you know which answer is correct. And the last two answers are obvious— even if you hadn't studied at all, you'd know that the last Indian group to come to North America must be "Eskimos," not "buffalo."

Did you notice that item *e* is a little bit tricky? If you had started with that phrase, you might have thought the answer should be the name of an Indian tribe, not an animal. Now that you've filled in the other answers, of course, you can see that it means the buffalo were hunted on the Great Plains. And when you stop to think about it, you know that neither the Mound Builders nor the Eskimos (the two groups of Indians in the list) lived on the Great Plains. But this is a good example of how you can get confused if you don't take time to look over the whole question.

Did you try the sample matching lists on your own before reading the explanation? What answers did you get? Here are the correct ones: *1 = b; 2 = d; 3 = f; 4 = e; 5 = a;* and *6 = c.*

Be sure to read the directions carefully for matching-list questions so you'll know what you're supposed to do. For instance, sometimes the two lists have the same number of items so that each one matches up with only one from the other list. But sometimes one list is longer than the other. Are you supposed to use some items twice, or are there items that won't be used? Don't go crazy trying to guess about this—find out before you start.

ESSAY QUESTIONS

Many students dread the idea of answering an essay question. They seem to think it's much harder than other kinds of test questions. An essay question does take more time to answer, and you have to think through what you're going to write. But really, writing a short essay gives you a chance to show how well you've learned the material for the class. And it's the only time you get to express your own opinion on a test—that can be a lot of fun!

As in the other sections of a test, it's important to read the instructions for an essay question carefully. You need to know exactly what is required in your answer. For instance, look at this question: "Which country contributed most to the exploration of the New World? Give reasons for your answer." It won't be enough simply to write down the name of a country in your answer—you have to explain why you chose that one.

In a question like this, it's up to you to decide what you think is the best answer. You might think Spain contributed most, or England, or maybe France. What facts do you know that back up this opinion? Your answer will be based on the material you've studied in class and in homework assignments. When you write your essay, you will have to use the facts you've learned to support the opinion you are giving.

FOUR STEPS TO SUCCESS

It's not hard to write a good answer to an essay question. Just follow these four steps:

1. *Think through what you want to say* in your essay. It's worth taking time to get your ideas organized in your mind before you start writing, even if your answer will be only one paragraph.

2. *Jot down quick notes* or a very brief outline on the back of your test paper—this keeps you from forgetting what you've planned to say.

3. *Write your answer in complete sentences and state things as clearly as you can.* Pretend you are explaining your ideas to someone who knows nothing at all about the subject. This helps keep you from leaving out important information.

4. *Try to finish in time to read over your essay* before the bell rings. It's easy to leave out letters or whole words when you're writing a test answer, and you'll want to fix any mistakes so your teacher won't have trouble knowing what you meant to say.

BEFORE YOU HAND IT IN

Whatever kind of test you're taking, it's a good idea to go back and check your paper before you hand it in. You may find answers that are too sloppy to be read; you may find questions you forgot to answer; you may find careless errors that need to be corrected. Now is the time to fix all these little problems. It's even possible that as you go through your test one more time, you'll suddenly come up with an answer you couldn't remember earlier.

But what if, no matter how well you tried to plan things, time is up and you haven't finished the test? There are still some questions you didn't get to or you're in the middle of writing your essay. What should you do?

First of all, write on your test, "I ran out of time here." This won't improve your test score, but at least it will let your teacher know why you didn't answer all the questions. And if this happens on more than one test, it's probably something you should discuss with your parents and your teacher. Maybe there is a way you can take your tests without a time limit. Some schools allow students to do this, and it's worth asking about if you have a lot of trouble finishing your tests on time.

If you're in the middle of an essay question when time runs out, it's a good idea to jot down an outline for the rest of your answer. This will take only a moment since you already have notes written down. Copy them quickly at the end of your paper so the teacher will know what you planned to say to complete your essay.

TAKE A DEEP BREATH, THEN RELAX

Do you still feel nervous when you think about taking tests? Remember that the only purpose of a test is to measure how much you've learned about a particular subject. Your teacher isn't trying to trick you or trap you with impossible questions. So if you've done your homework and paid attention in class, you'll do fine on your test.

CHAPTER 8

MAKE IT EASY ON YOURSELF

IS THERE ANYTHING ELSE THAT can help you do your best work in school? Yes, there is, and this may surprise you—it's your attitude.

When you think about it, it makes sense that your attitude toward school plays an important part in how much you get out of it. If you're enthusiastic and cheerful in class, your classmates and your teacher are likely to catch your positive outlook.

On the other hand, if all you do is talk about how "boring" everything in school is, you're not giving yourself a chance to find school interesting and even exciting. Maybe your schoolwork is boring to you because you think it's going to be boring before you even start. Why not try a new approach? After all, you have to go to school whether you want to or not, so you might as well make it as much fun as you can!

How can you tell if you have a good attitude in class? One of the most important things is participation. Do you speak up in class discussions? Some students are embarrassed to say anything in front of the whole class. They think they'll sound stupid or they'll stumble over their words. It doesn't help much to have someone say, "Don't be so shy." But it does help to remember that at least half of your classmates feel the same way you do. They'll admire your bravery in contributing to discussions. And the teacher will be pleased to have more people adding their thoughts and ideas—it makes class more interesting.

As for sounding stupid, have you ever heard the saying "The only stupid question is the one you don't ask"? That's a roundabout way of saying that it's stupid *not* to ask a question if you don't understand something. And it's true. Chances are that if you are confused about something, you're not the only one in class who feels that way. It's much better to raise your hand and ask for an explanation now. That way you won't be completely mystified by everything that follows.

Participating by joining in class discussions and by asking questions when you're not sure what's going on not only helps you keep up with class work, it also makes the time you spend in class more enjoyable. In addition, it lets the teacher know you're paying attention. This is important. Teachers spend a lot of time preparing for their classes, and they're only human. They get annoyed when they feel no one is bothering to listen.

WHAT ELSE ANNOYS TEACHERS?

You probably already know the answer to that question. The same kinds of things that make your parents crazy make teachers tear their hair out, too. So if you want to get the most out of school with the least fuss and bother, here are some things NOT to do:

- show off how smart you are by shouting out answers or putting down other people's answers;
- push, shove, and act rowdy in class;

- come late and/or unprepared for class;
- make up feeble excuses for lateness or for doing poorly on tests—no one likes to listen to whining, and besides, that creative streak can be put to better use in your work for class!

You know from your own experience that it's more fun to do things with someone who's enthusiastic and who seems to be enjoying whatever is going on. Your teacher feels the same way. Try volunteering the next time a class project comes up. You may discover that it's a lot more interesting than you expected, and it will let your teacher know that you're doing more than just sleeping through class.

PROBLEMS WITH TEACHERS

What if you try your best to be cheerful and cooperative but you feel your teacher doesn't like you? Sometimes this happens. There are people whose personalities just don't seem to go together very well, and you may be in one of those situations.

Probably you won't be able to change to another class, so it's best to make up your mind to put up with it for this year. Next year will no doubt be better. And there are things you can do to make this school year more pleasant.

First of all, think about how you act in class. Is there something you're doing—chewing your gum noisily, interrupting other people, or whatever—that irritates your teacher horribly? It may not be really obvious, but if your teacher has said, "One more sarcastic comment from you and it's curtains," you should have a clue to what's annoying him or her. Maybe you can change your behavior in this one area, and when your teacher sees that you're trying, it will make things a lot better.

Another way to improve things is to ask your teacher for help with something you don't understand. Naturally, this is the right step whenever you have a problem in any of your classes, but it can be very hard to do if you feel a teacher doesn't like you. However, get your nerve up and ask the teacher for an appointment either before or after school.

When you get there, explain what it is that you're having trouble with, and be prepared to listen carefully. It isn't easy to take this first step, but try hard not to be nervous or afraid. You may be surprised at how kind your teacher can be. And once you've made it clear that you want to do the best you can in the class, it's likely that things will improve.

IS SOMETHING ELSE WRONG?

What if you have a different kind of problem? You get along fine with your teacher, but you're falling behind in your schoolwork. You try as hard as you can, but you just can't seem to keep up. What should you do?

The first thing to remember is that it's not your fault. If you've really been trying to do your schoolwork and you just can't get a grasp on it, maybe you're going about it the wrong way. You may feel embarrassed or ashamed that you're having trouble. But it probably won't help just to keep trying harder by yourself. You need some help.

Have you had a conference with your teacher? Maybe there is some little piece of information you missed when you were sick with the flu. Or maybe it's something more basic that you need assistance with. Sitting down with the teacher and working through the problem area can make clear to both of you what you're doing wrong. And once you get it straightened out, you'll be back on track.

Sometimes problems aren't so easily solved, but

don't give up. Keep looking for help. Maybe you need to talk to your parents or an older brother or sister. They care about you, and since they know you so well, they may be able to spot the problem in the way you're thinking about your schoolwork. And if they can't figure it out, they'll be able to find someone who can.

BEING SCHOOL SMART

School isn't just a matter of getting good grades. It's the place where you spend a lot of your time and where you see your friends. Maybe you joke around and say that gym and recess are your favorite subjects. But did you ever think that math and science and social studies and language arts are gym class for your mind? And doing well on a test is just as exciting as scoring the winning goal in a game. Schoolwork can be a lot of fun if you give yourself a chance to be school smart!

INDEX

ABOUT THE AUTHORS

Elizabeth James graduated from Colorado College with a B.A. in mathematics. In addition to her books for young readers, she has written screenplays, as well as nonfiction and novels for adults. She lives in Beverly Hills, California.

Carol Barkin received a B.A. in English from Radcliffe College. Formerly a full-time editor of children's books, she now does freelance editorial work when she's not writing. She lives in Hastings-on-Hudson, New York.

Ms. James and Ms. Barkin wrote plenty of school reports and book reports when they were in school, and they have applied the methods of research and writing that they learned then to create the nearly forty books they have written together. Since they live on opposite ends of the country, their collaboration also requires a lot of organizational skills!